I0098758

SALZKAMMERGUT POEMS

by

William Ruleman

Copyright ©2016 William Ruleman.

Cover painting, *View of the Traun*, copyright ©2016 William Ruleman.

Cover design by Anne Ruleman Barach.

ISBN 978-0-9978881-1-9 (Cedar Springs Books)

IN DEDICATION

to my loving and patient wife

ACKNOWLEDGMENTS

The author is grateful to the following journals, in which several of the poems in this book first appeared:

Ezra for "Blesséd Hour"

The Galway Review for "Obertraun" (published as "A Village in the Salzkammergut")

The Pennsylvania Review for "The Koppenbrüllerhöhle"

The Penwood Review for "The Krippenstein"

The Poetry Church for "Mountain Descent"

The Sonnet Scroll for "Sonnet of the Soul"

The Springs of Helicon for "The Buhlerbach" and "The Traun"

Tears in the Fence for "Below the Hoher Dachstein"

CONTENTS

INTRODUCTION

The following collection of poems stems from a journey that the poet and his wife took to the area near Hallstatt in the Salzkammergut in May of 2009. As such, it provides only a glimpse of part of a much greater region, one often overlooked by American tourists, perhaps, yet one that is rich in natural resources, history, and culture. Though the poet hopes to return to the region someday, "[f]led is that music" for now, as Keats says at the end of "Ode to a Nightingale," but "I shall sing a sweeter song tomorrow," to quote Theocritus by way of Coleridge in his note on "Kubla Khan."

The translations presented here are of verse by the Empress Elizabeth of Austria (1837-1898), known more popularly as "Sisi," as well as her fellow Austrian poets Karl Adam Kaltenbrunner (1804-1867) and Hugo von Hofmannsthal (1874-1929), all lovers of the Salzkammergut.

PREFACE

At first I had meant this to be a travel book.
At first I had meant to venture somewhere new,
Come back and tell my readers where to look
For all the greatest things to see and do.
This aim I had in mind. It only took
The going there to take a different view.
Only in traveling there did I realize
That all must see the world with their own eyes.

Yet deeper was the wish to go somewhere
Where we had never been, my mate and I—
To force ourselves to take a risk and dare
Do something dangerous before we die—
Dangerous for us, who tend to take such care
To groove the rut of our routines and shy
Away from all that is unexpected, strange.
So we needed something to make us make a change.

My love had longed to take a walking tour
In Ireland, but the costs seemed high for us,
The paths remote, the routes to them unsure,
Requiring tedious plans for car or bus.
We sought a cure for our complex lives—a pure
And simple journey short on muss and fuss.
Checking guide after guide, route after route,
At last we settled on the Salzkammergut.

Salzkammergut—"Salt Chamber Estate"—domain
Of nobles who made their weary minions mine
The salt of that earth in poverty and pain,
Yes, kept them tethered there through shrewd design—
Inbreeding in that realm of rocks and rain,
Their yield ensuring the wealth of the noble line
That numbered lunatics among the sane—
Or so our guide said, though little did we care:
We saw the Dachstein and simply had to go there,

That mountain that Princess "Sisi" had found enchanting,
Stifter too; no, rather than sit and relax,
We longed to trudge up trails that would leave us panting,
Though we cared less about historic acts
And devilish dates than what our hearts were feeling,
No, found no satisfaction in files of facts:
For wanderers are less the writers of histories
Than seekers awed by Earth's dark mysteries.

THE APPROACH

As I recall, we raced through a land
Of lulling hills that lured us both
Toward sleep until the train slipped down
A vale unveiling a weird new world
Where lakes and mountains loomed all round—
Scintillant seas, wrinkled rocks
Laved in lavender, laced with mist
And fragile firs that fastened to them
For love of their lives while red-tiled roofs
And sailboat masts assailed the sky.

Right. I recall how we rose and paced
The aisle of that almost empty train
With dread that we could not drink it all in,
Pressing our knees to the seats as we peered
Through window after window frame
To sate our souls with sights that left
Us feeling far less joy than fear
We would cease to breathe ere satisfying
Our craving for those cols' mad colors,
Those molten boulders' majesties.

Our longing lamed us more than we meant.
We collapsed against our knapsacks, sighing,
Resolving to act right and be more restful.
Tumbling off the train at our stop
And hiking toward our hotel that evening,
We felt disoriented, forlorn.
Yet life is one longing after the next.
Fagged by fatigue, we still seethed for a siege.
Daring a peek out our window at dusk,
We knew we must mount those heights the next morn.

THE DACHSTEIN

(after Elisabeth, Empress of Austria: "Sisi")

Had I the strength, I would set you right
Down in the sea, where harsh winds blow.
Only then would you see your splendid might
And endless embroidery of snow.

The North Sea would be your looking glass
Within whose waves, high and wild, you would see
Your noble features ever pass;
In them you would build your new dynasty.

She is worthy, the same in rank as you;
And so, in order to make her your own,
Receive her into your realm; ah, do,
You prince of every glacial throne!

OBERTRAUN

(16 May 2009)

> "I am certain that in some later epoch humanity will be as
> sensitive to noise as it now is to bad smells and that the most
> severe penalties and public reprimands will be given for
> violations of one's hearing."
>
> --Gustav Mahler, in a letter to Natalie Bauer-Lechner

> There are other places
> Which are also at the world's end . . .
>
> --T. S. Eliot, "Little Gidding"

This place, too, seems at the world's end.
The mountains dwarfing this little *Dorf*
Appear to *command* a quietude.
At times a sports car will rebel,
A motorcycle maim the calm;
Trains will trickle through, tame as toys,
Tiny 'neath the towering peaks;
In vain do they sustain much noise.

The *karst* crags seem to brood over one,
A gloomy Greek chorus, backdrop for
A dreary stage for unproclaimed pain,
And close their ranks at dusk, immense,
As in "Childe Roland to the Dark Tower Came."
Yet tragedy in the traditional sense?
For how could one hope for *hubris* here,
These goblins gobbling up every aim,
Every feeble fumble at manmade fame?

TO WANDERERS FROM AFAR

(after Karl Adam Kaltenbrunner)

Here on your cozy course throughout this land,
Refrain from rushing through your wanderings:
Inquire and linger! Heed not just the things
The main path shows you, close at hand.

So you may find the joys this place has planned
For you, and so the songs the poet sings
Do not deceive you, seek the pleasurings
Of Alpine crowns where hearts, like skies, expand.

This proud domain, shut off by walls of stone,
Is craved by man, who pushes boldly on
Through gorge and wild whose greetings loom austere.

Not to say the beauty is concealed.
And yet it may require to be revealed.
For our winning, then, stand these stern heights here!

THE KRIPPENSTEIN

(17 May 2009)

And on the precipice,
And on the grassy mead,
With endless shouts and bliss,
Now let the roaming proceed!

--Joseph von Eichendorff, "Wandering for All"

Loth to believe what we so grieved to hear,
For still we had hopes that pointed to the clouds,
We questioned him again, and yet again;
But every word that from the Peasant's lips
Came in reply, translated by our feelings,
Ended in this, that we had crossed the Alps.

--William Wordsworth, *The Prelude*

Near the Five Fingers Overlook

The whole world seems to be wandering on
This Sabbath day atop this stone
Still glacier-graced, despite the heat:
Yes, all around me, wandering feet,
And mine, like theirs, I guess, should feel
It all routine. Yet it seems unreal.
I'm stricken with *Sehnsucht*—longing for more—
A yearning to pass through that sacred door
Where all's revealed and I'm at one
With God and cloud and snow and sun,
So I fidget, fret this way and that
For several moments (shy of the hat
That would guard my crown from the sun's subtle burn);
I roam and hither and thither turn,
Seeking via ceaseless motion
To summon the requisite emotion.

14

And stumbling on, I start to seem
A sleepwalker caught in webs of dream,
Not William Ruleman on the Krippenstein
But someone else. *These* legs? Not mine.
Not mine, these hands, eyes, ears, and breath.
My single self has died a death
Unawares as on that stony ground
I seem to fuse with all around.

Yet I could not keep on savoring this.
Like Wordsworth on that pass, my bliss
Was undercut by a sense of regret,
Though while he felt the Alps in his debt,
My own insatiable ecstasy
Suggested something deficient in *me*.

THE HEILBRONNERKAPELLE

Selig sind die, die keine Gewalt anwenden; denn sie werden das Land erben.

--Matthäus 5.5

As we turned away from the five-finger overlook
With its view of the valley, lake, and town below
And mountain ranges that rolled on and on as if
Reflected in an endless hall of mirrors,
A small chapel up the slope made us curious
Yet only deepened my sense of self-distrust.
Why enter this wretched place of worship here,
This meager and feeble dwelling built by man
Amid this superhuman spacious splendor
Except for refuge from its dwarfing power,
Escape from my own yearnings and inadequacy?

Yet as I entered the dark and humble room,
I bowed my head, surrendered to its gloom,
And thought of the hikers who had died on these heights
In a blizzard decades ago, their last days and nights
Upon our earth spent roaming a chill form of hell
Within the throes of a lingering winter's spell;
And mountain spirits seemed to speak to me
As I considered that modern tragedy.

THE ELEMENTS IN UNISON:

Humans built this chapel here
In memory of a little band
Whose leader did not know the land
And learned too late the need to fear

The ways of water, earth, and air
And how (they say) we may conspire
To stifle any man's desire
To conquer us—to his despair.

Warned thrice that day of certain storm—

16

In town, then on the slopes and peak—
He had no wish to be shown weak
So forced his troops to show fine form.

The thirteen in his charge that day—
A little school group seeking fun
On mountain heights in fresh spring sun—
Discovered, to their deep dismay,

A blizzard of relentless force,
Which all would march against in vain
And all because of his insane
Insistence that they stay the course.

1ˢᵗ MOUNTAIN SPIRIT (EARTH):

Good Friday, 1954:
They made a Calvary of my hill,
Submitting to their Judas' will
To suffer as One had before.

2ⁿᵈ MOUNTAIN SPIRIT (AIR):

I wafted round as rescuers tried
To save them from a frost-fraught fate;
They found them, but, alas, too late:
By then, the entire party'd died.

1ˢᵗ MOUNTAIN SPIRIT (EARTH):

I would have given them warm berth,
But water, air, wished otherwise;
I shuddered as snow filled the skies.
I am just poor Mother Earth.

3ʳᵈ MOUNTAIN SPIRIT (FIRE):

Absolve me, too, of any blame:
I would have helped them if I could
But how, alas, with ice-laced wood?

17

I sputtered, could not summon flame.

2nd MOUNTAIN SPIRIT (AIR):

Many cried out in their grief.
My winds caught up and saved those cries
Which still soar nightly in the skies.
My chill at last gave death's relief.

1st MOUNTAIN SPIRIT (WATER):

I wished to melt, was not in the mood.
Something made me mad, perverse.
Air's interference made things worse.
Icy, I could only brood,

Watching blinding snowflakes flit.
Mesmerized by marble clouds
That sailed the air like funeral shrouds,
Some met their deaths not knowing it.

1st MOUNTAIN SPIRIT (EARTH):

Oh miserable man, I'm not your slave.
You thought to master me, subject
Me to a flippant disrespect.
Mistreated so, I could not save.

THE ELEMENTS IN UNISON:

Please know that *all* of us care but are bound
By powers, laws we must obey,
So future guests should mind that they
Traverse a strange and sacred ground.

CHORUS:

Did some protest? Were they shouted down,
Cowed by a demon who deemed he could conquer nature,
A coward hellbent on proving himself

At the cost of twelve other humans' lives,
Driving his minions on like machines
Through prideful dearth of humility,
Contempt for the natural fact of cold
And the workings of the elements?

Those who seek to exalt themselves
Through daring feats or fancy allusions
Can run the risk of becoming lost,
So blinded by their abilities,
So dazed by their dash and derring-do,
Because of ego's dazzling snow,
They forget their fellow woman and man,
Reject the sense of what is plain
For the sorriest village fool to see,
The facts of God's reality.

COUNTER-CHORUS:

Yet might he have hoped that they be strong—
Tougher than he had ever been—
So pushed them ever onward, along
And felt no trace, no sense of sin,
Of the pride that ate him up inside
And proved the reason why they died?

Or was his some pantheistic view
That nature would accommodate,
Caress and comfort—despite what we do?
They learned the lie of this too late—
Learned too late she is not our nursemaid,
Learned too late to admire, respect.

MYSELF:

All of this I did not think then.
Yet I sensed that this was a holy place,
Sensed this as we left the sun
And entered the dark and cramped little den
Where over the altar, in German, Christ's words

19

"Blesséd are the meek" are inscribed,
And all at once I was filled with calm.

"Blesséd are the meek" (those old, worn words)
"For they shall inherit the earth." Indeed.
Yet the substitution of *land* for *earth*
Made me read these words as never before.

The meek *shall* inherit the earth, for they
Are at one with her, have never left her,
Have never forsaken her for the lures
Of the city and all its false appeal,
Or, if forced away from her,
Living lives divorced from her,
Tucked away in cities where they
Have never known the expanse of sky
And views as from these heaven-touched heights,
Even if they have rejected her
For the insane snares of the world we all know,
They shall nonetheless return to her
With a sense of peace as their one true home.

And she shall receive them with open arms
And a spirit free of resentment, regret,
For she needs them in order to be complete.

BLESSÉD HOUR

(after Hugo von Hofmannsthal)

Here where I lie, sans house or tent
Seems the world's peak, the firmament!

The ways of people lie all around me,
Up to the mountains, down to the sea.

They bear the goods that please them so;
Each holds my life, though none would know.

From rushes, grass, they bring, on wings,
Fruits I long lacked, life's dearest things.

These figs I know; now I sense the spot:
Still living, those things I long forgot!

And for me it was life, snatched from my hand,
Kept in the sea and kept in the land!

BELOW THE HOHER DACHSTEIN

I look on high;
Has some unknown omnipotence unfurled
The veil of life and death? Or do I lie
In dream, and does the mightier world of sleep
Spread far around and inaccessibly
Its circles?

--Percy Bysshe Shelley, "Mont Blanc"

His words returned as I gazed up at you,
Inhuman height forbidding mortal feet.
Though not as high as his Mont Blanc, you greet
Us with an ever all-too-daunting view.

And vain, our efforts to evade your stare,
Our fruitless thrusts at fun and food and drink
Down in that café on the Dachstein's brink,
Your looming presence up above us there

Remote as in some grainy classic film,
Yes, like an image cast upon a screen
As backdrop to our bland and cozy scene:
Sheer dream it seemed to us, your icy realm.

But then, the rescue dogs tied up nearby
Reminded us once more that you were real,
Admonished us to think and feel
That we were feeble creatures and would die.

And too, the fir trees felled by glaciers, tossed
About the Dachstein's slopes on our descent,
Brought back the poet's strange and sad lament:
"So much of life and joy is lost."

22

MOUNTAIN DESCENT

(Hugo von Hofmannsthal)

Descending wide paths where the mountain's flow ebbs,
I felt I was lying in wonderful webs—
The webs of God—caught in life's dream;
I heard the birds sing; I heard the winds stream.

How the vale wore the gems of the waters' spill!
How the forest stirred; how it swelled, the hill!
A falcon flew high in the still heavens' gleam:
My heart lay in life, in death, in dream.

ALONG THE RIVER TRAUN

The felled firs on the slopes had filled me
With vague restlessness, a brooding gloom,
Yet leaving the cable car to climb
Our way to the river through the woods,
I was touched by the day's tranquility,
The gentle heat, and, save for the calls
Of birds, a silent calm. We were safe
From nature's dangers, I decided,
In this landscape like that near our home
In the tender hills of east Tennessee.
The firs, the sun, the heat made us feel
At home, indeed, though soon, vague doubt
Seeped into my thoughts as I recalled
How we had chased the Cherokees from
Their homes in our own Holocaust
Historians term the Trail of Tears.
And now, at once, worn out and sad,
I sensed myself a stranger here.

We passed a young man pushing a pram,
Then some elderly codger clad
In swimming trunks and sweeping the path
That led to a shed—as if a sheer
Dirt path required such dainty care!
Neither party paid us heed . . .
Oh, we were utter aliens here,
Nothing if not non-entities!
And then, new signs of nature's darkness:
Crude paintings tacked to boards on trees
To mark the memories of the Traun's
Crass unconcern and treachery
For ones who had loved and lived beside her:
A lumberjack the currents lunged
To his doom one fine and destined day,
A twelve-year-old girl caught up in its swirl—
Both drowned in the torrents. My terror returned,
As did my sadness; I suddenly knew

24

We are all of us wanderers in this world;
The earth is not our home at all;
The best we can hope for are moments of beauty
And love and kindness and comfort and calm
While, ever hounded by horrors and awe,
We hold fast to our faith in some future day
When this lovely and strange yet dangerous realm
Will be Eden again, that place of peace
We rightly seek. Already I sensed
That these violent, seemingly vengeful waters,
Wilder by far than Wordsworth's Wye,
Would yet, like that river he revered,
Give "life and food for future years."

THE TRAUN

These swirling pale green waters flow
Forever on and do not cease;
One knows the restlessness they know;
One also feels their inner peace.

We know ourselves as strangers here;
This is not our homeland; yet
This swirling pale green river here
I will not easily forget:

It lingers in my memory
And urges me to make this rhyme
And so becomes a part of me,
This ceaseless river, mocking time.

THE BUHLERBACH

(20 May 2009)

Secluded in a shaded nook,
Your presence takes us by surprise,
An *Ursprung* spread to sundry springs,
A lulling lingo in ten tongues
Delighting open ears and eyes
With gurgling, spurting spouts in stone
That give each *Wasserweg* its tone
As, slipping down rocks' slickened rungs,
It slaps and sometimes claps along,
Spatters, clatters as it sings
And lends notes to this lovely song,
This liquid book called lovers' brook.

THE HALLSTÄTTERSEE

(Karl Adam Kaltenbrunner)

The shadows fall from the rocks' immensity
Down from the heights upon your glassy face;
The dark waves rest with deep and quiet grace;
A shudder of the sublime comes over me.

I saw the sharp walls fall, and I could see
Eternal crags enveloped in a lace
Of mist and felt within my heart the trace
Of a great and still and sad profundity.

And yet that grayish painting starts to clear,
And from the murky field you start to peer
Upon the lucid human houses there,

Which clamp themselves against the mountain hem,
Glad to let their roofs encoffin them
As avalanches threaten, storm skies glare.

HALLSTATT AND THE ECHERNTALWEG

We took the ferry across the lake to the town
And saw the painted skulls in the bone house there,
Observed the mountain stream come crashing down
To fill the fount from which I drank my share.
We sought the *Waldbachstrub*, a waterfall
On a way that led from the town into the wood.
I wandered on with no concern at all
Until my love said we were lost. I understood
Her thirst for surety, her gnawing need
To know where we were, so asked two Austrian gents
If they thought the pathway we were on would lead
To the waterfall. Though their answer made no sense
To me, I still took the path they recommended,
Though wonder even now where our trek might have ended,

For how can another ascertain the way
To proceed in this, our journey through this life?
Every dog must dictate his own damned day,
Carve out the rut that suits his own strange strife.
To take the course that others claim is best
May reap success, yet at what psychic cost?
We ache, we chafe, we know a rank unrest:
Some part of us still wishes we were lost.

And so it was for me as we headed back
The way we had come to take a different path—
I heard the birds sing yet felt a certain lack
Of self-regard that well-nigh turned to wrath
Until that roaring foam made me forget
The prideful thoughts that had made me fume and fret.

THE WALDBACHSTRUB

(Karl Adam Kaltenbrunner)

Darkness fell. All cheer had fled the scene.
I stood engulfed by gloomy, looming trees;
Thunder shocked me from my reveries
In your rugged, crude, and weird ravine.

Many a one who's traveled far and wide
Is mightily stirred by your wild vale's spacious home,
Has gazed upon your waters' raging foam
As on the cruel blaze of the ocean's tide.

Your crags shake not before the might of men;
The elements four are boundless in your ken;
Though you were molded from mere granite rock,

A path was drilled through your immensity;
A font was scooped where your shudder seizes me;
And torrents spray from your dark depths with a shock!

ADALBERT STIFTER ON THE ECHERNTALWEG

Your *Frau* was destined never to bear a child,
And you saw several kindred's offspring die
In senseless ways that meant to drive you wild
With sadness. Fatal sickness, suicide—why?

But just as God appears to call some home
Before their time for reasons yet unclear,
So might He send to Earth from Heaven's dome
Angelic beings to help us bear life here.

At first they seemed less mortal children than fairies
As they approached you on the path that day,
But when they tried to sell you their strawberries,
You felt it wrong to send them on their way

But bought their fare, which you commanded they eat;
And as you watched them prance about and dance,
Those little mountain *Kinder* at your feet,
Were you already seeing your romance

Concerning some cold and stormy Christmas Eve
With brother and sister caught in nature's lair?
And since your childless fortune sought reprieve,
You could not bear to let them die up there,

But had them hunted down, retrieved, and saved,
To fight the lack that might have left you depraved.

31

SONNET OF THE SOUL

(Hugo von Hofmannsthal)

A thousand creatures' pulsing will
Rages inside us like racing horses;
Veins' vines seethe; wildfire courses
Throughout us and lures us to hurt and kill.

Battle-tested bestial forces,
Well-selected manly skill
Suit our hell. And so we spill
Our legacy of Earth's resources.

Yet listening to our souls, we hear
Ice start to clink, and water stir,
And then strange currents, loud and clear,

And then a wingbeat's quiet whirr.
And we feel ourselves alone
With earthly powers we had not known.

THE KOPPENBRÜLLERHÖHLE

(20 May 2009)

"Come, God-denier, and feel Him now . . ."

--Nikolaus Lenau, "Wandering in the Mountains"

Crude congeries of cave-spewed streams
(Tumbling, crashing, splashing, spraying
From deep in the Dachstein with mounting might),
You surge ever onward, ever conveying
Courage, fear, dread, delight.
All our worries, scoldings, schemes?
Deafened in your incessant roar;
Trifles drown before your door.

Yours, good friend, an ever-humbling
Arrogance-stifling roar and thunder,
Cure for our day's cacophony,
Reminder there is still terror and wonder,
Nurture in nature's symphony,
Grim antidote to our petty grumbling
And death to the trivial tyranny
Of tedious technology!

Yet while you humble, you also exalt,
Soothe one with your surfeit of sound,
Send one into a stupid state
That is, in turn, so wise and profound
We lose all longing to preen and prate,
To squander our seconds in finding fault
With siblings or self yet feel, in this place,
Hushed awe as your rapids roil and race!

Yours—gleaming, gushing—the word of God,
Which wakens while it mesmerizes,
Withering sin with its wordless song,
Its monotone drone that shocks and surprises,
Warning in waves our warped world's wrong,

33

Censuring me, some silly sod
Who, with weak words, could hardly dare
Provide some sense of your wild wizard's prayer.

ABOUT THE AUTHOR

William Ruleman's previous books include three collections of his own poems, *From Rage and Hope* from White Violet Books and *A Palpable Presence* and *Sacred and Profane Loves* (both from Feather Books), as well as the following volumes of translation: *Poems from Rilke's Neue Gedichte* (WillHall Books, 2003), *Vienna Spring: Early Novellas and Stories* of Stefan Zweig (Ariadne Press, 2010), and, also from Cedar Springs Books, *Verse for the Journey: Poems on the Wandering Life* by the German Romantics, *A Girl and the Weather* (poems and prose of Stefan Zweig),and *Selected Poems of Maria Luise Weissmann*. His individual poems and translations have appeared in many journals, all over the world.

www.ingramcontent.com/pod-product-compliance
Lightning Source LLC
Chambersburg PA
CBHW061759040426
42447CB00011B/2377